Weight Loss Smoothies: 101 I
Gluten-free, Sugar-free, Dai
Smoothie Recipes to Help You L.....

by **Alissa Noel Grey**
Text copyright(c)201 Alissa Noel Grey

All rights reserved. No part of this publication may be reproduced, distributed, or transmitted in any form or by any means, including photocopying, recording, or other electronic or mechanical methods, without the prior written permission of the publisher, except in the case of brief quotations embodied in critical reviews and certain other noncommercial uses permitted by copyright law

Although every precaution has been taken to verify the accuracy of the information contained herein, the author and publisher assume no responsibility for any errors or omissions. No liability is assumed for damages that may result from the use of information contained within.

Table Of Contents

Smoothies That Melt Belly Fat

Spring is the time of year when most of us start thinking about our weight loss goals. In my family we usually start this season by making a slow transition to a lighter and healthier diet and adding more fresh fruit and vegetables in our everyday menu. The easiest way to do this is by having a delicious smoothie for a snack or replacing breakfast or dinner with a smoothie. My fresh-tasting smoothies, with a little of bit of superfood seeds, nuts and herbs added, are packed with healthy nutrients, fiber and vitamins and will keep your metabolism active all day long. They will also curb your appetite by naturally maintaining healthy blood sugar levels and will help you lose a few pounds without even trying very hard.

The weight loss smoothies in this book are balanced, filling and taste great, and you don't need to count calories when you prepare them. They will keep you full, help you avoid cravings and over-eating, and burn fat at the same time. You can replace one or two meals a day with a delicious smoothie for weight loss, or add it to your regular diet routine for weight maintenance and wellness.

Strawberry and Coconut Smoothie

Serves: 2

Prep time: 2-3 min

Ingredients:

2 cups frozen strawberries

1 cup coconut milk

1 tbsp coconut butter

1 nectarine, chopped

Directions:

Combine all ingredients in a high speed blender and blend until smooth.

Revitalizing Tomato Smoothie

Serves: 2

Prep time: 2-3 min

Ingredients:

1-2 cubes frozen spinach

3 tomatoes, cut

1 carrot, chopped

½ celery rib, chopped

½ cup mint leaves

a pinch of salt and black pepper

Directions:

Combine all ingredients in a high speed blender and blend until smooth.

Detox Support Smoothie

Serves: 2

Prep time: 2-3 min

Ingredients:

1-2 ice cubes

1 cup water

½ avocado, chopped

2 carrots, chopped

1/2 raw beet, peeled and chopped

1/2 lemon, juiced

black pepper and salt, to taste

Directions:

Combine all ingredients in a high speed blender and blend until smooth.

Peach and Cucumber Smoothie

Serves: 2

Prep time: 2-3 min

Ingredients:

2-3 ice cubes

1 small cucumber, peeled and chopped

1/2 banana, peeled and chopped

1 large peach, chopped

Directions:

Combine the ice, water, banana, peach and cucumber in a high speed blender. Blend until smooth and serve.

Chamomile, Peach and Ginger Smoothie

Serves: 2

Prep time: 2-3 min

Ingredients:

4-5 ice cubes

1 cup chamomile tea

1 lime, juiced

2 large peaches, chopped

1 tsp grated ginger

Directions:

Combine all ingredients in a high speed blender and blend until smooth.

Strawberry and Arugula Smoothie

Serves: 2

Prep time: 2-3 min

Ingredients:

2 cups frozen strawberries

1 cup unsweetened almond milk

10-12 arugula leaves

1/2 tsp ground cinnamon

Directions:

Combine ice, almond milk, strawberries, arugula and cinnamon in a high speed blender. Blend until smooth and serve.

Emma's Amazing Smoothie

Serves: 2

Prep time: 2-3 min

Ingredients:

1 frozen banana, chopped

1 cup orange juice

1 large nectarine, sliced

1/2 zucchini, peeled and chopped

2-3 dates, pitted

Directions:

Combine all ingredients in a high speed blender and blend until smooth.

Good-To-Go Morning Smoothie

Serves: 2

Prep time: 2-3 min

Ingredients:

1 cup frozen strawberries

1 cup apple juice

1 banana, chopped

1 cup raw asparagus, chopped

1 tbsp ground flaxseed

Directions:

Combine all ingredients in a high speed blender and blend until smooth.

Endless Energy Smoothie

Serves: 2

Prep time: 2-3 min

Ingredients:

1 frozen banana, chopped

11/2 cup green tea

1 cup chopped pineapple

2 raw asparagus spears, chopped

1 lime, juiced

1 tbsp chia seeds

Directions:

Combine all ingredients in a high speed blender and blend until smooth.

High-fibre Fruit Smoothie

Serves: 2

Prep time: 2-3 min

Ingredients:

1 frozen banana, chopped

1 cup orange juice

2 cups chopped papaya

1 cup shredded cabbage

1 tbsp chia seeds

Directions:

Combine all ingredients in a high speed blender and blend until smooth.

Nutritious Green Smoothie

Serves: 2

Prep time: 2-3 min

Ingredients:

2-3 frozen broccoli florets

1 cup apple juice

1 large pear, chopped

1 kiwi, peeled and chopped

1 cup spinach leaves

1-2 dates, pitted

Directions:

Combine all ingredients in a high speed blender and blend until smooth.

Apricot, Strawberry and Banana Smoothie

Serves: 2

Prep time: 2-3 min

Ingredients:

1 frozen banana

11/2 cup almond milk

5 dried apricots

1 cup fresh strawberries

Directions:

Combine all ingredients in a high speed blender and blend until smooth.

Spinach and Green Apple Smoothie

Serves: 2

Prep time: 2-3 min

Ingredients:

3-4 ice cubes

1 cup unsweetened almond milk

1 banana, peeled and chopped

2 green apples, peeled and chopped

1 cup raw spinach leaves

3-4 dates, pitted

1 tsp grated ginger

Directions:

Combine all ingredients in a high speed blender and blend until smooth.

Superfood Blueberry Smoothie

Serves: 2

Prep time: 2-3 min

Ingredients:

2-3 cubes frozen spinach

1 cup green tea

1 banana

2 cups blueberries

1 tbsp ground flaxseed

Directions:

Combine all ingredients in a high speed blender and blend until smooth.

Zucchini and Blueberry Smoothie

Serves: 2

Prep time: 2-3 min

Ingredients:

1 cup frozen blueberries

1 cup unsweetened almond milk

1 banana

1 zucchini, peeled and chopped

Directions:

Combine all ingredients in a high speed blender and blend until smooth.

Tropical Spinach Smoothie

Serves: 2

Prep time: 2-3 min

Ingredients:

1/2 cup crushed ice or 3-4 ice cubes

1 cup coconut milk

1 mango, peeled and diced

1 cup fresh spinach leaves

4-5 dates, pitted

1/2 tsp vanilla extract

Directions:

Combine all ingredients in a high speed blender and blend until smooth.

Mango and Cucumber Smoothie

Serves: 2

Prep time: 2-3 min

Ingredients:

1/2 cup crushed ice or 3-4 ice cubes

1 cup coconut milk

1 mango, peeled and diced

1 small cucumber, peeled and chopped

1-2 dates, pitted

1 tbsp chia seeds

Directions:

Combine all ingredients in a high speed blender and blend until smooth.

Pear and Spinach Smoothie

Serves: 2

Prep time: 2-3 min

Ingredients:

2-3 frozen spinach cubes

1 cup orange juice

2 large pears, peeled and chopped

1 tsp ground flaxseed

Directions:

Combine all ingredients in a high speed blender and blend until smooth.

Kale and Kiwi Smoothie

Serves: 2

Prep time: 2-3 min

Ingredients:

2-3 ice cubes

1 cup orange juice

1 small pear, peeled and chopped

2 kiwi, peeled and chopped

2-3 kale leaves

2-3 dates, pitted

Directions:

Combine all ingredients in a high speed blender and blend until smooth.

Detox Fennel Smoothie

Serves: 2

Prep time: 2-3 min

Ingredients:

1 cup frozen pineapple

1 cup water or green tea

1 small fennel, chopped

½ cucumber, chopped

1 lime, peeled

Directions:

Combine all ingredients in a high speed blender and blend until smooth.

Pomegranate and Fennel Smoothie

Serves: 2

Prep time: 2-3 min

Ingredients:

1 frozen banana

1 cup pomegranate juice

1 small fennel, chopped

1 pear, chopped

1 lime, juiced

Directions:

Combine all ingredients in a high speed blender and blend until smooth.

Delicious Broccoli Smoothie

Serves: 2

Prep time: 2-3 min

Ingredients:

2-3 frozen broccoli florets

1 cup coconut milk

1 banana, peeled and chopped

1 cup pineapple, cut

1 peach, chopped

1 tsp cinnamon

Directions:

Combine all ingredients in a high speed blender and blend until smooth.

Papaya Smoothie

Serves: 2

Prep time: 2-3 min

Ingredients:

2-3 frozen broccoli florets

1 cup orange juice

1 small ripe avocado, peeled, cored and diced

1 cup papaya

1 cup fresh strawberries

Directions:

Combine all ingredients in a high speed blender and blend until smooth.

Beet and Papaya Smoothie

Serves: 2

Prep time: 2-3 min

Ingredients:

3-4 ice cubes

1 cup orange juice

1 banana, peeled and chopped

1 cup papaya

1 small beet, peeled and cut

Directions:

Combine all ingredients in a high speed blender and blend until smooth.

Lean Green Smoothie

Serves: 2

Prep time: 2-3 min

Ingredients:

1 frozen banana, chopped

1 cup orange juice

2-3 kale leaves, stems removed

1 small cucumber, peeled and chopped

1/2 cup fresh parsley leaves

½ tsp grated ginger

Directions:

Combine all ingredients in a high speed blender and blend until smooth.

Easy Antioxidant Smoothie

Serves: 2

Prep time: 2-3 min

Ingredients:

2-3 frozen broccoli florets

1 cup orange juice

2 plums, cut

1 cup raspberries

1 tsp ginger powder

Directions:

Combine all ingredients in a high speed blender and blend until smooth.

Healthy Purple Smoothie

Serves: 2

Prep time: 2-3 min

Ingredients:

2-3 frozen broccoli florets

1 cup water

1/2 avocado, peeled and chopped

3 plums, chopped

1 cup blueberries

Directions:

Combine all ingredients in a high speed blender and blend until smooth.

Delicious Fennel Smoothie

Serves: 2

Prep time: 2-3 min

Ingredients:

1/2 cup crushed ice or 2-3 ice cubes

1 cup apple juice

1 cup chopped fennel

1 large pear, chopped

2-3 dates, pitted

1 lime, juiced

Directions:

Combine all ingredients in a high speed blender and blend until smooth.

Mom's Favorite Kale Smoothie

Serves: 2

Prep time: 2-3 min

Ingredients:

2-3 ice cubes

1½ cup orange juice

1 green small apple, cut

½ cucumber, chopped

2-3 leaves kale

½ cup raspberries

Directions:

Combine all ingredients in a high speed blender and blend until smooth.

Creamy Green Smoothie

Serves: 2

Prep time: 2-3 min

Ingredients:

1 frozen banana

1 cup coconut milk

1 small pear, chopped

1 cup baby spinach

1 cup grapes

1 tbsp coconut butter

1 tsp vanilla extract

Directions:

Combine all ingredients in a high speed blender and blend until smooth.

Mojito Smoothie

Serves: 2

Prep time: 2-3 min

Ingredients:

1 cup crushed ice

1 cup coconut milk

1 large apple, chopped

3 limes, peeled and cut

10 fresh mint leaves

Directions:

Combine all ingredients in a high speed blender and blend until smooth.

Winter Power Smoothie

Serves: 2

Prep time: 2-3 min

Ingredients:

2 broccoli florets, frozen

1 cup orange juice

1 banana, peeled and chopped

½ cup chopped pumpkin

1 apple, chopped

2 kale leaves

2-3 dates, pitted

Directions:

Combine all ingredients in a high speed blender and blend until smooth.

Dark Green Veggie Smoothie

Serves: 2

Prep time: 2-3 min

Ingredients:

3-4 frozen spinach cubes

1 cup water

1 cup chopped kale, trimmed, chopped, tightly packed

1 banana, chopped

1 large apple chopped

1 pear, chopped

Directions:

Combine all ingredients in a high speed blender and blend until smooth.

Kale and Raspberry Smoothie

Serves: 2

Prep time: 2-3 min

Ingredients:

2-3 ice cubes

1 cup almond milk

1/2 avocado, pitted, peeled and chopped

3-4 kale leaves

2 cups raspberries

Directions:

Combine all ingredients in a high speed blender and blend until smooth.

Delicious Kale Smoothie

Serves: 2

Prep time: 2-3 min

Ingredients:

2-3 ice cubes

11/2 cups apple juice

3-4 kale leaves

2 figs, chopped

1 cup strawberries

Directions:

Combine all ingredients in a high speed blender and blend until smooth.

Healthy Apricot Smoothie

Serves: 2

Prep time: 2-3 min

Ingredients:

2-3 ice cubes

1 cup almond milk

1/2 avocado, peeled and chopped

4 apricots, chopped

1 apple, chopped

5-6 arugula leaves

Directions:

Combine all ingredients in a high speed blender and blend until smooth.

Cherry Smoothie

Serves: 2

Prep time: 2-3 min

Ingredients:

1 frozen banana, chopped

1 cup almond milk

2 cups pitted cherries

1 tsp cinnamon

Directions :

Combine all ingredients in a high speed blender and blend until smooth.

Banana and Coconut Smoothie

Serves: 2

Prep time: 2-3 min

Ingredients:

1 frozen banana, chopped

1 cup coconut milk

2-3 small broccoli florets

1 cup grapes

1 tbsp coconut butter

Directions :

Combine all ingredients in a high speed blender and blend until smooth.

Delicious Celery and Apple Smoothie

Serves: 2

Prep time: 2-3 min

Ingredients:

4-5 ice cubes

1 cup apple juice

1 large apple, chopped

2 celery sticks, chopped

1/2 cup diced pineapple

Directions:

Combine all ingredients in a high speed blender and blend until smooth.

Avocado and Pineapple Smoothie

Serves: 2

Prep time: 2-3 min

Ingredients:

3-4 ice cubes

1 cup orange juice

1 small ripe avocado, peeled, cored and diced

1 apricot, chopped

2 cups diced pineapple

Directions:

Combine all ingredients in a high speed blender and blend until smooth.

Carrot and Mango Smoothie

Serves: 2

Prep time: 2-3 min

Ingredients:

1/2 cup frozen mango chunks

1 cup carrot juice

1 carrot, chopped

1 large peach, chopped

1 tbsp raw cashews

1 tsp grated ginger

Directions:

Combine all ingredients in a high speed blender and blend until smooth.

Tropical Carrot Smoothie

Serves: 2

Prep time: 2-3 min

Ingredients:

1/2 cup frozen mango chunks

1 cup carrot juice

1 carrot, chopped

1 cup melon, chopped

1 tbsp shredded coconut

Directions:

Combine all ingredients in a high speed blender and blend until smooth.

Beautiful Skin Smoothie

Serves: 2

Prep time: 2-3 min

Ingredients:

1 cup crushed ice

1½ cup pomegranate juice

1 avocado, peeled, pitted and sliced

1 cup fresh strawberries

1 peach, chopped

Directions:

Combine all ingredients in a high speed blender and blend until smooth.

Pumpkin and Quince Smoothie

Serves: 2

Prep time: 2-3 min

Ingredients:

1 frozen banana, chopped

11/2 cup orange juice

1 large quince, peeled and chopped

1 cup pumpkin puree

Directions:

Combine all ingredients in a high speed blender and blend until smooth.

Banana, Walnut and Fig Smoothie

Serves: 2

Prep time: 2-3 min

Ingredients:

1 frozen banana

1 cup water

3 fresh figs, washed, stems removed, halved

2 tbsp walnuts

Directions:

Combine all ingredients in a high speed blender and blend until smooth.

Kiwi and Pear Smoothie

Serves: 2

Prep time: 2-3 min

Ingredients:

1/2 cup crushed ice

1 large pear, chopped

1 cup green tea

3 kiwi, peeled and halved

1 tbsp chia seeds

Directions:

Combine all ingredients in a high speed blender and blend until smooth.

Caribbean Health Smoothie

Serves: 2

Prep time: 2-3 min

Ingredients:

2-3 ice cubes

1½ cup almond milk

1 medium ripe avocado, peeled, cored and diced

1 mango, peeled, diced

1 cup pineapple, chopped

1 cup papaya

Directions:

Combine all ingredients in a high speed blender and blend until smooth.

Skinny Melon Smoothie

Serves: 2

Prep time: 2-3 min

Ingredients:

3-4 frozen broccoli florets

1 cup green tea

½ honeydew melon, cut in pieces

1 tsp ground flaxseed

Directions:

Combine all ingredients in a high speed blender and blend until smooth.

Healthy Skin Smoothie

Serves: 2

Prep time: 2-3 min

Ingredients:

1 cup frozen pear

1 cup almond milk

1 medium ripe avocado, peeled, pitted and diced

1 cup pumpkin puree

1 tsp vanilla extract

1 tsp cinnamon

Directions :

Combine all ingredients in a high speed blender and blend until smooth.

Paleo Diet Raspberry Smoothie

Serves: 2

Prep time: 2-3 min

Ingredients:

1 frozen banana

11/2 cup coconut water

2 cups raspberries

2 tbsp raw cashews

Directions:

Combine all ingredients in a high speed blender and blend until smooth.

Arugula and Peach Smoothie

Serves: 2

Prep time: 2-3 min

Ingredients:

1/2 cup crushed ice or 2-3 ice cubes

1/2 cup water

1 banana, peeled and chopped

10-12 arugula leaves

1 large peach, chopped

Directions:

Combine the ice, water, banana, arugula and peach in a high speed blender. Blend until smooth and serve.

Super Berry Smoothie

Serves: 2

Prep time: 2-3 min

Ingredients:

3-4 ice cubes

1½ cup green tea

1 medium avocado, peeled, cored and chopped

1 cup blueberries

½ cup blackberries

1/2 cup raspberries

Directions :

Combine all ingredients in a high speed blender and blend until smooth.

Fennel and Berry Smoothie

Serves: 2

Prep time: 2-3 min

Ingredients:

3-4 ice cubes

1½ cup orange juice

1 small avocado, peeled, cored and chopped

1/2 fennel, peeled and chopped

1 cup blueberries

½ cup blackberries

Directions :

Combine all ingredients in a high speed blender and blend until smooth.

Carrot, Banana and Walnut Smoothie

Serves: 2

Prep time: 2-3 min

Ingredients:

1 frozen banana

1 cup orange juice

2 carrots, chopped

1 tbsp raw walnuts

1 tsp grated ginger

Directions:

Combine all ingredients in a high speed blender and blend until smooth.

Rainbow Smoothie

Serves: 2

Prep time: 2-3 min

Ingredients:

1 cup frozen blueberries

1 banana, peeled and chopped

1 cup orange juice

1 kiwi, peeled and halved

1 tsp pumpkin seeds

Directions:

Combine all ingredients in a high speed blender and blend until smooth.

Mango and Almond Breakfast Smoothie

Serves: 2

Prep time: 2-3 min

Ingredients:

1 cup frozen mango chunks

1 banana, peeled and chopped

11/2 cup green tea

1 kiwi, peeled and halved

1 tbsp almond meal

Directions:

Combine all ingredients in a high speed blender and blend until smooth.

Kale and Date Smoothie

Serves: 2

Prep time: 2-3 min

Ingredients:

1 frozen banana, chopped

1½ cup coconut milk

1 nectarine, chopped

2-3 leaves kale

15 dates, pitted

Directions:

Combine all ingredients in a high speed blender and blend until smooth.

Kiwi and Grapefruit Smoothie

Serves: 2

Prep time: 2-3 min

Ingredients:

3-4 ice cubes

2 large pink grapefruits, juiced

1 banana, chopped

3 kiwi, peeled and halved

1 tbsp ground flaxseed

Directions:

Juice the grapefruit then combine the juice with all other ingredients in a blender. Blend until smooth.

Mango and Nectarine Smoothie

Serves: 2

Prep time: 2-3 min

Ingredients:

1/2 cup crushed ice or 3-4 ice cubes

1 cup orange juice

1 small ripe avocado, peeled, pitted and chopped

1 mango, peeled, diced

2 nectarines, chopped

Directions:

Combine all ingredients in a high speed blender and blend until smooth.

Carrot and Nectarine Smoothie

Serves: 2

Prep time: 2-3 min

Ingredients:

1/2 cup crushed ice or 3-4 ice cubes

1 cup unsweetened almond milk

1 banana, peeled and chopped

1 large carrot, chopped

2 nectarines, chopped

Directions:

Combine all ingredients in a high speed blender and blend until smooth.

Pineapple and Pear Smoothie

Serves: 2

Prep time: 2-3 min

Ingredients:

4-5 ice cubes

1 cup coconut milk

2 cups pineapple, chopped

1 large pear, chopped

1 small bunch parsley

Directions:

Combine all ingredients in a high speed blender and blend until smooth.

Delicious Vitamin Smoothie

Serves: 2

Prep time: 2-3 min

Ingredients:

4-5 ice cubes

1 pink grapefruit, juiced

1 large orange, juiced

1 small ripe avocado, pitted, peeled and chopped

1 carrot, chopped

1 plum, chopped

2-3 dates, pitted

2 tbsp walnuts

Directions:

Juice the grapefruit and the orange then combine with all other ingredients in a high speed blender. Blend until smooth.

Ginger Smoothie

Serves: 2

Prep time: 2-3 min

Ingredients:

4-5 frozen broccoli florets

1 cup carrot juice

1 lime, juiced

1 banana, chopped

1 apple, peeled and chopped

1 tsp grated ginger

Directions:

Combine all ingredients in a high speed blender and blend until smooth.

Peach and Avocado Smoothie

Serves: 2

Prep time: 2-3 min

Ingredients:

4-5 ice cubes

1 cup apple juice

1 small ripe avocado, peeled, pitted and chopped

2 peaches, sliced

1/2 cucumber, peeled and chopped

1 tsp ground ginger

Directions:

Combine all ingredients in a high speed blender and blend until smooth.

Detox Green Smoothie

Serves: 2

Prep time: 2-3 min

Ingredients:

3 frozen spinach cubes

1 cup orange juice

1/2 zucchini, peeled and chopped

1/2 yellow pepper, cut

1 banana, peeled and chopped

1 apple, chopped

½ lemon, juiced

8-9 fresh mint leaves

Directions:

Combine all ingredients in a high speed blender and blend until smooth.

Peach and Melon Green Smoothie

Serves: 2

Prep time: 2-3 min

Ingredients:

3-4 frozen broccoli florets

1 cup green tea

1/2 ripe avocado, peeled and chopped

1 cup honeydew melon pieces

1 peach, chopped

1 tsp ground flaxseed

Directions:

Combine all ingredients in a high speed blender and blend until smooth.

Melon and Cherry Smoothie

Serves: 2

Prep time: 2-3 min

Ingredients:

3-4 cubes frozen spinach

2 cups honeydew melon pieces

1 cup ripe cherries, pitted

1 tbsp coconut butter (optional)

Directions:

Combine all ingredients in a high speed blender and blend until smooth.

Raspberry and Broccoli Smoothie

Serves: 2

Prep time: 2-3 min

Ingredients:

2-3 frozen broccoli florets

1 cup pomegranate juice

1 banana, peeled and chopped

2 cups fresh raspberries

1 tsp vanilla extract

Directions:

Combine all ingredients in a high speed blender and blend until smooth.

Delicious Plum and Cherry Smoothie

Serves: 2

Prep time: 2-3 min

Ingredients:

3-4 ice cubes

11/2 cup almond milk

1/2 ripe avocado, peeled and chopped

3 plums, pitted and chopped

1 cup cherries, pitted

½ tsp cinnamon

Directions:

Combine all ingredients in a high speed blender and blend until smooth.

Pumpkin Pie Smoothie

Serves: 2

Prep time: 2-3 min

Ingredients:

1 frozen banana, chopped

1 cup coconut milk

1 large pear, peeled and chopped

½ cup pumpkin puree

½ tsp cinnamon

1 tsp vanilla extract

Directions:

Combine all ingredients in a high speed blender and blend until smooth.

Quince and Apple Smoothie

Serves: 2

Prep time: 2-3 min

Ingredients:

4-5 ice cubes

1 cup apple juice

1 large apple, chopped

1 ripe quince, peeled and chopped

1/2 tsp cloves

Directions:

Combine all ingredients in a high speed blender and blend until smooth.

Watermelon and Raspberry Smoothie

Serves: 2

Prep time: 2-3 min

Ingredients:

1 cup frozen raspberries

2 cups watermelon, seeded

6-7 raw almonds

Directions:

Combine all ingredients in a high speed blender and blend until smooth.

Watermelon and Spinach Smoothie

Serves: 2

Prep time: 2-3 min

Ingredients:

4-5 ice cubes

2 cups watermelon, seeded

2 cups baby spinach leaves

3-5 dates, pitted

Directions:

Combine all ingredients in a high speed blender and blend until smooth.

Watermelon Mohito Smoothie

Serves: 2

Prep time: 2-3 min

Ingredients:

5-6 ice cubes

2 cups watermelon, seeded

1 banana, peeled and chopped

1 lime, juiced

1 cup fresh mint leaves

Directions:

Combine all ingredients in a high speed blender and blend until smooth.

Simple Tomato and Beet Smoothie

Serves: 2

Prep time: 2-3 min

Ingredients:

1-2 ice cubes

3 tomatoes, cut

½ avocado

1/2 raw beetroot, peeled and chopped

1/2 lemon, juiced

black pepper and salt, to taste

Directions:

Combine all ingredients in a high speed blender and blend until smooth.

Sweet Potato and Banana Smoothie

Serves: 2

Prep time: 2-3 min

Ingredients:

1 frozen banana, chopped

1 cup almond milk

1 cup mashed cooked orange sweet potato

1/2 head butter lettuce

1 apple, chopped

Directions:

Combine all ingredients in a high speed blender and blend until smooth.

Blueberry and Zucchini Smoothie

Serves: 2

Prep time: 2-3 min

Ingredients:

1 cup frozen blueberries

1 cup hazelnut milk

1 banana, chopped

½ zucchini, peeled and chopped

1 tsp vanilla extract

1 tsp cinnamon

Directions:

Combine all ingredients in a high speed blender and blend until smooth.

Zucchini Breakfast Smoothie

Serves: 2

Prep time: 2-3 min

Ingredients:

1 frozen banana

1 cup orange juice

½ zucchini, peeled and chopped

2 apricots, chopped

1 tbsp chia seeds

Directions:

Combine all ingredients in a high speed blender and blend until smooth.

Apricot, Basil and Lime Smoothie

Serves: 2

Prep time: 2-3 min

Ingredients:

1 frozen banana

1 cup orange juice

3 apricots, chopped

1 lime, peeled and cut

3 fresh basil leaves

1-2 dates, pitted

Directions:

Combine all ingredients in a high speed blender and blend until smooth.

Banana, Orange and Zucchini Smoothie

Serves: 2

Prep time: 2-3 min

Ingredients:

1 frozen banana

1½ cup orange juice

1 zucchini, chopped

2-3 dates, pitted

Directions:

Combine all ingredients in a high speed blender and blend until smooth.

Strawberry, Fennel and Orange Smoothie

Serves: 2

Prep time: 2-3 min

Ingredients:

4-5 ice cubes

1 cup orange juice

1 cup fennel

2 cups strawberries

1 tsp ground flaxseed

Directions:

Combine all ingredients in a high speed blender and blend until smooth.

Lemon and Melon Smoothie

Serves: 2

Prep time: 2-3 min

Ingredients:

3-4 ice cubes

1 cup almond milk

1 cup honeydew melon

½ lemon, peeled

1 apple, chopped

1 tbsp fresh mint

Directions:

Combine all ingredients in a high speed blender and blend until smooth.

Melon and Passion Fruit Green Smoothie

Serves: 2

Prep time: 2-3 min

Ingredients:

2-3 frozen broccoli florets

1 cup orange juice

1/2 avocado, peeled

2 cups honeydew melon, diced

2 passion fruit

1 tbsp fresh mint

Directions:

Scoop the pulp of the passion fruits into a blender and add all other ingredients. Blend until smooth.

Green Tea Smoothie Recipe

Serves: 2

Prep time: 2-3 min

Ingredients:

1 frozen banana, chopped

1½ cup strong green tea

1 small pear, chopped

1 cup baby spinach

2-3 dates, pitted

Directions:

Combine all ingredients in a high speed blender and blend until smooth.

Raspberry and Mango Smoothie

Serves: 2

Prep time: 2-3 min

Ingredients:

2 cups frozen mango chunks

1 cup almond milk

1 cup raspberries

½ orange, peeled and cut

Directions:

Combine all ingredients in a high speed blender and blend until smooth.

Sour Cherry Smoothie

Serves: 2

Prep time: 2-3 min

Ingredients:

1/2 cup crushed ice

1 cup almond milk

2 cups sour cherries, pitted

1 pear, peeled and chopped

1 tbsp ground flaxseed

Directions:

Combine all ingredients in a high speed blender and blend until smooth.

Berry and Cabbage Smoothie

Serves: 2

Prep time: 2-3 min

Ingredients:

1/2 cup crushed ice

1 cup water

1 small banana, peeled and chopped

1 cup red cabbage

1 cup strawberries

1 cup blueberries

Directions:

Combine all ingredients in a high speed blender and blend until smooth.

Blueberry and Passion Fruit Smoothie

Serves: 2

Prep time: 2-3 min

Ingredients:

2-3 ice cubes

3 passion fruits

1 cup orange juice

1 banana

2 cups blueberries

1 tbsp ground flaxseed

Directions:

Scoop the pulp of the passion fruits into a blender and add all other ingredients. Blend until smooth.

Peach and Cabbage Smoothie

Serves: 2

Prep time: 2-3 min

Ingredients:

1 banana frozen, chopped

1 cup water

1 cup red cabbage

1 large peach, chopped

1 cup grapes

½ tsp cinnamon

Directions:

Combine all ingredients in a high speed blender and blend until smooth.

Mint Cabbage Smoothie

Serves: 2

Prep time: 2-3 min

Ingredients:

1 frozen banana, chopped

1 cup water

1 cup cabbage

1 kiwi, peeled

1-2 dates, pitted

2-3 fresh mint leaves

Directions:

Combine all ingredients in a high speed blender and blend until smooth.

Mediterranean Smoothie

Serves: 2

Prep time: 2-3 min

Ingredients:

4-5 ice cubes

1 cup water

2 apricots, chopped

3-4 fresh figs, washed and halved

2-3 almonds

Directions:

Combine all ingredients in a high speed blender and blend until smooth.

Citrus and Fig Smoothie

Serves: 2

Prep time: 2-3 min

Ingredients:

4-5 ice cubes

1 cup water

1 banana, peeled and chopped

3 fresh figs, washed, stems removed, halved

1 orange, peeled and cut

1 tbsp sesame seeds

Directions:

Combine all ingredients in a high speed blender and blend until smooth.

Pineapple and Fig Smoothie

Serves: 2

Prep time: 2-3 min

Ingredients:

2 cups frozen pineapple

1½ cup orange juice

2 fresh figs, washed, stems removed, halved

1 cup baby spinach

Directions:

Combine all ingredients in a high speed blender and blend until smooth.

Fig and Cucumber Smoothie

Serves: 2

Prep time: 2-3 min

Ingredients:

4-5 ice cubes

1½ cup coconut milk

1 banana, peeled and chopped

3-4 fresh figs, washed, stems removed, halved

½ cucumber, peeled and chopped

½ tsp cinnamon

Directions:

Combine all ingredients in a high speed blender and blend until smooth.

Sweet Beet Smoothie

Serves: 2

Prep time: 2-3 min

Ingredients:

1 cup frozen blackcurrants

1 cup apple juice

1 small raw beet, peeled and chopped

1 cup red grapes

4-5 dates, pitted

Directions:

Combine all ingredients in a high speed blender and blend until smooth.

Raw Beet Smoothie

Serves: 2

Prep time: 2-3 min

Ingredients:

1 frozen banana, chopped

1½ cup coconut milk

1 beet, peeled and cut

1 carrot, chopped

1 cup blueberries

Directions:

Combine all ingredients in a high speed blender and blend until smooth.

Pineapple and Grapes Smoothie

Serves: 2

Prep time: 2-3 min

Ingredients:

1 cup frozen pineapple

1 cup hazelnut milk

11/2 cup seedless grapes

½ banana, chopped

1 tsp ground flaxseed

Directions:

Combine all ingredients in a high speed blender and blend until smooth.

Green Kiwi and Grape Smoothie

Serves: 2

Prep time: 2-3 min

Ingredients:

2-3 frozen broccoli florets

1 cup water

½ avocado

3 kiwi, peeled and cut

1 cup seedless grapes

1 tbsp chia seeds

Directions:

Combine all ingredients in a high speed blender and blend until smooth.

Blackcurrant and Pomegranate Smoothie

Serves: 2

Prep time: 2-3 min

Ingredients:

1 frozen banana, chopped

1½ cup pomegranate juice

1 cup blackcurrants

2 kale leaves

Directions:

Combine all ingredients in a high speed blender and blend until smooth.

Red Currant Smoothie

Serves: 2

Prep time: 2-3 min

Ingredients:

2 cups frozen red currants

1½ cup water

2 ripe peaches, chopped

2-3 dates

Directions:

Combine all ingredients in a high speed blender and blend until smooth.

Red Currant and Broccoli Smoothie

Serves: 2

Prep time: 2-3 min

Ingredients:

2-3 frozen broccoli florets

1 cup unsweetened almond milk

1 cup red currants

1 cup strawberries

2-3 dates

Directions:

Combine all ingredients in a high speed blender and blend until smooth.

About the Author

Alissa Grey is a fitness and nutrition enthusiast who loves to teach people about losing weight and feeling better about themselves. She lives in a small French village in the foothills of a beautiful mountain range with her husband, three teenage kids, two free spirited dogs, and various other animals.

Alissa is incredibly lucky to be able to cook and eat natural foods, mostly grown nearby, something she's done since she was a teenager. She enjoys yoga, running, reading, hanging out with her family, and growing organic vegetables and herbs.

22357275R00064

Printed in Great Britain
by Amazon